WELCOME TO CONWY
THE STORY OF A HISTORIC TOWN

The view of the town and its castle from Mynydd Conwy

First edition: 2004
New edition: 2013

© Gwasg Carreg Gwalch

ISBN: 978-1-84527-453-5

Cover design: Carreg Gwalch

Published by Gwasg Carreg Gwalch,
12 Iard yr Orsaf, Llanrwst, Wales LL26 0EH
tel: 01492 642031
fax: 01492 641502
email: books@carreg-gwalch.com
website: www.carreg-gwalch.com

The town walls and the estuary

Carreg Gwalch Guides

Welcome to
Conwy

The Story of a Historic Town
by Owain Maredudd

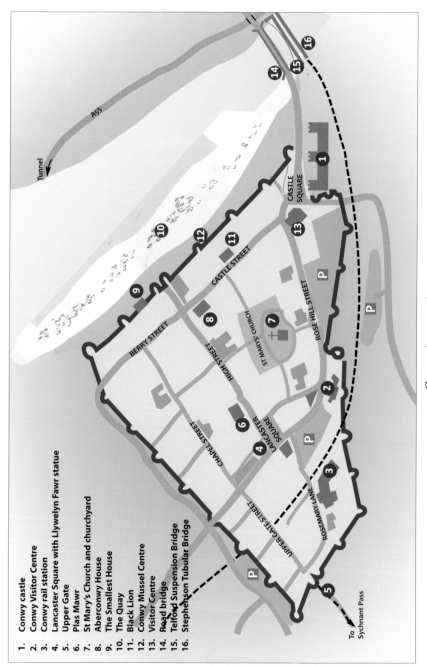

1. Conwy castle
2. Conwy Visitor Centre
3. Conwy rail station
4. Lancaster Square with Llywelyn Fawr statue
5. Upper Gate
6. Plas Mawr
7. St Mary's Church and churchyard
8. Aberconwy House
9. The Smallest House
10. The Quay
11. Black Lion
12. Conwy Mussel Centre
13. Visitor Centre
14. Road bridge
15. Telford Suspension Bridge
16. Stephenson Tubular Bridge

Conwy town centre

Contents

The historic town of Conwy

On a few occasions, the memory of a town and its locality will linger for a lifetime – and Conwy is such a town. First impressions are often misleading and a newcomer to the shores of Conwy estuary will easily be forgiven for believing that Conwy town story begins and ends with the building of its castle and its well-preserved town walls.

It is certainly a majestic castle, but Conwy's tidal waters had been a haven and a frontier for centuries before its short military service to the Norman kings. The quay quickly grew to be mightier than its towering fortress and the former colony evolved to be a significant market town and a river port servicing the Welsh heartland that at one time it was meant to tame.

Today, the colours of history are alive on the estuary waters, the narrow, renovated streets, the historic houses – there are over 200 listedbuildings within its walls – and the lively quayside. The past was built in layers and a wealth of depth is felt under the skin of present-day Conwy.

The annual 'Honey Fair' at Conwy, held every September

Conwy castle from one of the river crossings

The Celtic hill-fort on Mynydd Conwy

Lost lands and new worlds

Myths sometimes hold truths that are lost in historical facts and scientific studies. Near Conwy, earlier inhabitants lived in Brythonic villages, Celtic hill-forts, Bronze Age settlements and prehistoric caves. Over the centuries, they shared a common heritage which was handed down in an oral tradition in their Celtic/Brythonic language. This was later filtered through into the inheritance of the Welsh descendants of these earlier people, and today the Welsh language holds the key to a very old culture.

An important part of that culture was literature – epic legends and well-crafted poetry. Nearly always, these were based on old tribal memories and are signposts to pieces of lost histories. Welsh medieval literarture in the princes' courts of Gwynedd (the province of north-western Wales), re-echoed the tales that were told around the fires of circular Celtic hut-dwellers on Mynydd y Dref, behind Conwy, and even in the prehistoric caves of Y Gogarth – called the *Great Orme* by the Vikings, as it resembled a sea serpent from their longships.

Scientific research certifies that old tree stumps revealed at the lowest tides on sandy banks between Penmaenmawr and Llandudno are the remains of a submerged forest, 7,000 years old. Out there also are boulders aligned at regular angles: a formation called 'Llys Helig'. Geological deposits? Old weirs?

Legend has it that this was once the fine court of Helig ap Glannawg, lord of the lowlands. His daughter's lover murdered a young nobleman for the want of his golden torc. He then heard whispers '*Dial a ddaw, dial a ddaw*' ('revenge will come, revenge will come'). Four generations later, during singing and dancing in a great feast in Llys Helig, a maid discovered fish swimming in the cellar when she went for more wine. The sea dykes had broken and by the following morning, a bay of sea water covered all the lush lands of Helig and his court lied submerged forever – apart from those brief moments of low tide, which were enough to keep the legend alive through the ages (see Michael Senior's *Llys Helig and the myth of lost lands*).

Historians, generally, agree that sea-adventurers from Japan or Europe visited the American continent long before Columbus. Madog was the youngest son of Owain Gwynedd, a 12th century ruler of northern Wales. He preferred the sea to the mountain rocks, and learned seafaring skills from fishermen and merchants. Tired of war on the mainland, he sailed westwards, where the Celts always believed lied the Land of the Forever Young. He set sail from the mouth of Afon Ganol, beyond Deganwy hills to the east of Aberconwy. After many years, his ship reappeared over the horizon. He and his followers had found a great new land in the west and he appealed for volunteers to settle there. He then captained a fleet of ten ships and sailed for America for the last time.

Footholds yielded, new opportunities gained – these myths hold the essence of Conwy's history.

The dominant view from Mynydd Conwy over the Morfa and the estuary

The old entrance through the enormous stone walls of the hill-fort

The mouth of Afon Ganol – Aber Cerrig Gwynion

Caerhun – the site of old ford crossing Afon Conwy

The church at Caerhun, built on the site of the Roman fort

Roman eagles and Welsh dragons

Slowly, the Romans pioneered a road along the northern coast of Wales and crossed Afon Conwy about 3 miles upriver of Conwy town. Here they built a fort to guard the ford and the port: Caerhun.

Other Roman interest in the area were the copper mines on Y Gogarth above Llandudno, where they further exploited prehistoric works, and the pearl mussels of the river bed. They claimed that Conwy pearls were the largest and most beautiful throughout the British Isles. Occasional pearls have been found in Afon Conwy down the centuries – the last one in 1953.

The Romans left these lands at the mercy of foreign hordes but a strong leader, Cunedda, defended Welsh shores against attacks. From him, the ancestry of the royal line of Wales may be traced. In that line stands Maelgwn Gwynedd (died 549) who had his seat of power on the two hills above Deganwy, on the eastern bank of the Conwy estuary. He fought and won a famous battle on the sandy dunes of Morfa Rhiannedd, where the streets of Llandudno were laid down thirteen centuries later. After the death of King Arthur in 546, Maelgwn was elected the king of the Welsh to carry on the resistance against the Anglians and Saxons and was known as 'the Dragon of the Island'.

He was also strong in cunning. He claimed superiority on other chieftains in northern Wales following a canute-style contest at Abedyfi. Each rival brought his throne to the water's edge and whoever held out longest against the incoming tide would be declared an overlord. The other proud leaders brought their ceremonial thrones, decorated with heavy metals and stones. Maelgwn brought a simple seat of goose-quills and wax and as he floated above the rest, so was the hierarchy of the kings of Deganwy secured.

Tradition has it that Maelgwn surrounded himself with poets and in his court was held the earliest record of a Welsh Eisteddfod (a cultural event where poets, musicians and singers display their talents and compete). Under the king's patronage, a congress of bards and musicians was held at Deganwy castle. Maelgwn decided that a competition between the two crafts was to be held on Mynydd y Dref, above Conwy. Any boats had been previously hid and all the competitors had to swim across Afon Conwy before the contest. As a result, the harps and pipes were useless and the poets – favoured by Maelgwn, of course – carried the day.

One of Maelgwn's poets prophecised that the Welsh would 'praise their lord, keep their language and lose all their lands – except the wild terrain of Wales'. During the king's lifetime, Saxon and Germanic tribes had already established themselves in eastern Britain. Vikings would soon be on the horizon. But Maelgwn had established a dynasty that would secure the safety of Gwynedd which would set an example and vision that would occasionally unify the whole of Wales to stand against invaders.

The twin hills above Deganwy – the site of the Welsh castle

One of the few remains of Deganwy castle

Deganwy hills viewed across the estuary from Conwy town walls

The estuary near Cymryd ford, on high tide

The mud and sand bank on the diagonal ford of Cymryd, the site of the Welsh victory known as 'Dial Rhodri' ('Rhodri's revenge)

16

Strength and survival

For centuries, the story of Conwy's estuary was the history of Wales. It was contested but not conquered; snatched but never surrendered. Vikings attacked from the western sea; Anglians and Saxons from the east and the wooden fort of Deganwy was destroyed by lightning in 810.

But an able leader was found in Rhodri, who guarded his shores with a fleet of warships. The Vikings were to kill all the royal families of England – bar Wessex – and occupy expansive territories there, but were denied a foothold in Wales. Rhodri defeated the Vikings in 856, killing Horm their king, and gained an international reputation. He united the whole of Wales as one nation and became known as Rhodri Mawr – the first in Welsh history to carry the title 'the Great'.

He was killed in battle in 878, but his sons carried on with his work, defeating the Anglians of Mercia for the last time in a battle at Cymryd near Conwy three years later. It became known to the Welsh as '*Dial Rhodri*', Rhodri's revenge.

A new invader extended his shadow across Afon Conwy after 1066. The Norman earl, Robert of Rhuddlan, built a new stone castle at Deganwy around 1080 but again Gwynedd rose – under Gruffudd ap Cynan this time – who landed three ships at Deganwy as Robert was cut down by Welsh spears in the battle which followed.

The Normans were driven by the same greed and power that had already seen the whole of England succumb in a few months. The Anglo-Saxons leaders were decimated forever, the serfs became second-class citizens. Theirs was not the language of law or government.

Wales, in the same period, saw a burst of military and literary activity. Poets sang in Welsh for their princes, recording their deeds, indicating also that there was a national renaissance and a new political awareness. Gruffudd's son, Owain, extended the territory of Gwynedd to the English border, consolidating his gains by building castles. Henry II assembled a great army at Oswestry in 1165 and attacked Wales, but was met by an united Welsh force from every corner of Wales. Foul weather and hard terrain demoralized Henry's army. He retreated, burning churches, mutilating hostages. Seeds of further bitterness were sown.

Fathers passed on bows and spears to sons and often the guerilla tactics of the Welsh grinded down armies that outnumbered them. Foreign mercenaries hardly dared to cross Afon Conwy and challenge the mountain fortress of Eryri (*Snowdonia*) and for centuries, the river was a natural moat keeping the enemy at bay.

Deganwy, however, was on the eastern side of the river and exchanged hands many times during the conflict as armies approached along the strip of lowland along the coast of north-eastern Wales. The Welsh kept their distances at times, resisted fiercely when the opportunity came, kept the river as a final line of defence and survived.

A historic plaque at Deganwy castle

The view over the estuary and Conwy bay from Deganwy

Conwy from Deganwy

The central statue of Llywelyn Fawr in the square

The stone cask of Llywelyn – originally at Aberconwy Abbey,
now at Capel Gwydir in Llanrwst church

The abbey of Aberconwy

Greatness in a king is traditionally extended by later generations – it is not a contemporary title handed out by a desire to please a ruling monarch. After Rhodri and Owain, a third great leader hailed from Conwy shores – Llywelyn Fawr (*the Great*).

His statue stands in the old market square of Conwy today, carrying his full name, Llywelyn ap Iorwerth. On 24 July, 1186 he gave a charter to Cistercian monks to establish an abbey – which stood at the site of Conwy's parish church today. He also gave them sea-weir, wrecking and ferry rights, land on Y Gogarth and mountain pastures.

Llywelyn also erected a hall (its remains are part of the town walls today) as a royal palace for himself at Aberconwy, as the abbey was called (aber: *estuary*). Llywelyn, after unifying and securing Wales with many famous victories over the Normans, spent his last years within the abbey walls. When he died in 1240, he was interred in front of the high altar. When Edward I evicted the monks from their privileged lands to Maenan to make room for his colonial town, the faithful men took Llywelyn's stone coffin with them. After the Dissolution, it was removed again and now reposes, minus lid and occupant, in Capel Gwydir, Llanrwst parish church.

The abbey was not destined for a quiet, peaceful life however. Twice, King John of England, invaded the district, burning the cathedral at Bangor, but spared Aberconwy abbey. In 1245, Henry III and his army were trapped on the eastern side of the river. Greedy for plunder, 300 rowed across the river, pursued the Welsh and spoiled the abbey of Aberconwy, burning the books and other treasures belonging to it. It robbed Wales of a wealth of archives, literature and historical information.

The abbey became the mausoleum of princes – Gruffudd and Dafydd, Llywelyn Fawr's sons were also laid to rest here. But war was always at its doorstep. Prince Edward of England garrisoned

Deganwy castle and another Llywelyn, the grandson of Llywelyn Fawr, besieged it reduced them to eating the flesh of their own horses and dogs in 1263. Edward surrendered, Deganwy was destroyed forever and in the following treaty Llywelyn ap Gruffudd was confirmed as the prince of the whole of Wales.

But Edward was ruthless and ambitious. His treachery was described by a contemporary English writer by the words: 'When he is cornered he promises whatever you wish but as soon as he is free he forgets his promise.' For a whole year, Edward prepared in detail and at a great cost three huge armies to invade Wales. He forced Llywelyn back to Eryri and a treaty was signed in Aberconwy in 1277, striping the Welsh ruler of most of his lands. Another Welsh War of Independence followed, but Llywelyn was killed by a stray soldier on the banks of Irfon in central Wales. Llywelyn's head was carried on a spear through the streets of London.

Edward's army crossed Afon Conwy and in January 1283 captured the Welsh stronghold of Castell Dolwyddelan in the heart of Eryri.

Dolwyddelan castle – a Welsh strongland upriver

St Mary's church, Conwy

Stones from the old abbey at Aberconwy are found at the foot of the bell tower

Conwy castle from the river

The Snowdonian backdrop to the Fortification

A castle for a king

Conwy is dominated by its castle. Today, old and ruined, it has an elegant beauty above changing tides and against a backdrop of mountain scenery. Every year, thousands of fascinated visitors walk through its gateway and climb its towers.

There is no doubt that it was a building feat in its day. Edward I arrived in Conwy in March 1283 and within four days of his arrival, arrangements were made to work on new fortifications on the western side of Afon Conwy, securing a foothold on Eryri's shore. Master engineers, an army of craftsmen and labourers and the services of James of St George, the greatest military architect of the age, were all enlisted in the building of a castle and a walled town that took only four and a half years to complete.

It was a part of a Plantagenet fortresses scheme in northern Wales built to symbolise Norman dominance and subdue the Welsh. It was the largest, most expensive construction programme in medieval Europe. More than 1,500 workers – mostly drawn from all over England – were employed at Conwy alone.

The castle itself is pinned on a rock above the river, and defended by three walls on its western side. The eight drum towers are massive in their strength – it is a compact, great mass of solid masonry created to defend a king's ambition.

A charter was granted to the town on 8 September, 1284 and special favours were extended to encourage English settlers. The Welsh were banned from buying land or a house or from holding any office in the town and were only let in for the weekly market, to buy and sell goods at English prices. The aim was to deposses the Welsh of their lands, their commerce, their resources, language and heritage.

The castle's elaborate defences however, betray the weakness of Edward I's position – nowhere else in his territories was such protection called for. Its strategy was to defend a foothold rather than to conquer the whole of Eryri. Originally, it was whitewashed to catch the sunlight and draw attention to its standards, there, within reach of the dark mountains. No doubt it also attracted the glare of any Welsh people who would view it from the distance.

On more than one occasion, the invaders were extremely grateful for its physical sturdiness. In 1294-5, Madog ap Llywelyn of royal Welsh blood, led a revolt against the castle towns, burning Caernarfon and besieging Conwy. Edward was trapped in his own masonry in its castle, cut off from his army and his provisions. Here the proud king was obliged to live on water and a little honey until the danger passed.

In the end, these castles are stone skeletons which testify to hollow victories and are, by today, sources of pride in their own resilience to the Welsh people who are now responsible for their upkeep. A restoration programme was started in 1953 and by 1987 the castle and the town walls of Conwy – together with Beaumaris, Caernarfon and Harlech – are inscribed on the World Heritage List as a historic site of outstanding universal value.

Inside the great hall

The strong towers, showing traces of whitewash

Additional defences

The walls running to the river front to defend the port of Conwy

Most of the town is still within the old walls

A town behind walls

Conwy town maintained its medieval harp-shape for centuries – it did not outgrow its town walls until 20th century estates were built at Gyffin and on Sychnant road. It still constitutes one of the best-preserved castle and walled towns in Europe.

It was, like other fortress towns in northern Wales, a garrisoned island which could be comfortably supplied from the sea. For centuries, the Welsh countryside was considered too dangerous for any infiltration by government officials or even armed forces that were not exceptionally strong in numbers. Wales outside the walled towns lived a life of its own, but behind the strong stonework Welsh laws and customs were prohibited. A free borough was granted to the burgesses of Conwy and adventurers and speculators from England and France were invited to settle here. Trading and racial rights were thrown at them. As local historian Christopher Draper puts it: 'The castle and walled town were the chosen device for producing and enforcing a new, loyal, ethnically-cleansed settlement' (*Walks from Conwy*).

The privileged, fortified township was challenged by generations of Welsh uprisings. After Madog's revolt of 1294-5, the Welsh awaited for Owain Lawgoch – a Welsh prince in exile who fought as a French captain against the English. His 1372 fleet, sailing for Wales, was hampered by bad weather and an English assassination terminated his life in Montagne-sur-Gironde in 1378.

In 1400, the charismatic Owain Glyndŵr led a revolt which saw every foreign castle and town in Wales attacked as he laid down the foundations of modern Wales with his vision of an independent government, church and university. In the spring of 1401, Gwilym and Rhys ap Tudur, Anglesey noblemen, brothers in arms and forefathers of Henry Tudor of Wales, besieged Conwy's walls. On Good Friday, while the garrison soldiers were in church, the gateway had been wedged open by a rebel sympathiser and the

Welshmen captured the castle without shedding a drop of blood and burnt the town and its mill. The unthinkable had happened! An English army marched on the town and attacked the castle, but all in vain. Finally, when their provisions ran low the Welsh left the town through negotiation, surrendering nine hostages to the English. They left and Glyndŵr's campaign went from strength to strength, but the nine hostages were promptly executed.

Conwy again saw action and its garrison was thoroughly demoralised during the long years of Owain Glyndŵr's campaign. The valley was wasted during the War of the Roses when the Earl of Pembroke led a great army through Eryri and then a temporary peace followed. The influence of the fortress receded and the old alien family names died out. Early records are full of Hookes, Robinsons, Burches and Porters but by Tudor times, Welsh families were established within Conwy's town walls. The colony had passed away; Conwy from then onwards is a Welsh town.

Tŵr Llywelyn – part of the Welsh hall incorporated in Edward's walls

*A heavily defended gateway to Conwy town
and the conveniences high on the walls*

Conwy walls – one of the best examples of medieval town walls in Europe

Tŷ Aberconwy

'Ffair Fêl' – the annual honey fair

Tŷ Aberconwy and other old buildings

One of the best known houses in Conwy is 'Tŷ Aberconwy', standing on one of the original plots that lined Castle Street and High Street, now a National Trust property. It is traditionally dated at 1400 and might have survived the destruction of Glyndŵr's uprising; on the other hand it was possibly built from the ashes after the Tudur brothers put the town to the torch in 1401. Either way it is the best surviving example of a medieval town house in northern Wales.

It was once the home of a successful merchant and the ground floor was used as a bakery and a fish and chip shop, among other things. Today, it has been restored to its past glory, with a National Trust shop in the basement and the upper two floors housing an audio-visual presentation showing the daily life of Conwy through different periods of its history, with furnished rooms displaying traditional Welsh furniture on loan from the Museum of Welsh Life.

Originally, Conwy was a town of a few streets and many gardens and was well-known for its herbs, flowers, fruits and honey. Two of Conwy's traditional fairs continue to be held to this day, Ffair Hadau (*Seed Fair*) on 26th March and a Ffair Fêl (*Honey Fair*) on 13th September. The name of Berry Street, leading northwards from Tŷ Aberconwy however is misleading – it was originally Burial Street where the dead of the 1607 plague were buried in the street. Workmen were to find bones here when digging up the road at a later date and a large number of skeletons were revealed when part of High Street was lowered and repaired.

Further up Castle Street from Aberconwy House is the striking building, the old Black Lion – a vicarage at one time, it still displays a memorial stone with the inscription '1589 I.B.E.'. It was built in that year for Vicar John Bricknall (I being the Latin form of J) and his wife Em. Later it became a tavern, a coaching inn and an antique shop. Every Monday morning a pig market used to be held there. On Castle Street also is the much-altered Old College building (now a menswear shop). It is said to have its foundations in the old abbey of Aberconwy and was later extensively remodelled but fragments of it could be the oldest parish stone walls in the town.

The beautiful parish church of St Mary is the oldest building in the town, incorporating the remains of the abbey in the west wall of its tower, including three lancet windows. As the town prospered in the later Middle Ages, the church enjoyed its share of good fortune. The great eastern window was erected in the chancel, the font was built in Tudor times and the tower was raised. Its rood screen is particularly impressive – it used to accommodate singers and musicians as well as a small organ.

The churchyard also includes many interesting features – a sundial, the 'we are seven' grave of Wordsworth fame as well as seats for a tranquil moment to take in the beauty and the historic connections.

The 'We are seven' grave in Conwy churchyard

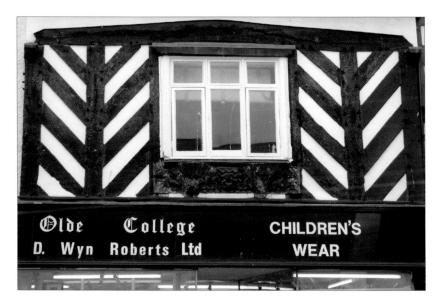

The Olde College, Castle Street

The old 'Black Lion'

Plas Mawr, a Tudor town house

The Flemish influence

The Welsh gentry of Plas Mawr

Plas Mawr was built between 1576 and 1585 for Robert Wynn – a Welshman and a member of the Wynn family that had already established itself on an estate around its home at Castell Gwydir, Llanrwst. The family had already gained power and land by careful politics during the early Tudor era, and acquired the property of Abaty Aberconwy (then at Maenan) at the Crown's dissolution of the monasteries. Robert Wynn was a remarkable and well-travelled trader and belonged to the class of Welsh gentry who gave personal profits before Welsh patriotism during the Elizabethan era. He had, however, an European flair and many features of Plas Mawr display his continental connections.

Plas Mawr is noted for its ornamental plasterwork, many of it embellished by various crests, shields and arms of the old kings and princes of Wales, as the Wynns traced their ancestry back to early royal bloodlines with pride. The three eagles of Owain Gwynedd are seen here, the 'three severed Englishman's heads' of Ednyfed Fychan, Grand Forester of Eryri; the fleur-de-lys of Collwyn ap Tango, lord of Eifionydd and Ardudwy and the red dragon of king Cadwaladr and Henry VII. It is rich in ornamentation, the finest surviving town house of the Elizabethan era to be found anywhere in Britain. It was authentically renovated at the end of the 20th century, which included restoring and repainting the original plasterwork and lime-rendering the outside walls.

The beauty of the building today is the effect of the blend in its design of the traditional halls of the local Welsh gentry and the Renaissance style features that Robert Wynn encountered on his European travels. In many ways, Plas Mawr would not look out of place in the historic towns of Flanders or the Netherlands, but the oak beams and slate roofing give it a distinct Welsh flavour. Robert Wyn died in 1598 and was buried in the parish church, after a good life in Conwy 'where he kept worthy plentiful house all his time'.

Plas Mawr was the home of the Royal Cambrian Academy from 1886 until recently – it is now housed in the former Congregational Chapel nearby. The RCA promoted artists in Victorian Conwy and was established at a meeting in a Llandudno Junction hotel in 1881.

Turning left into Chapel Street from Crown Lane, which runs alongside Plas Mawr, a vacant plot with stone memorials is reached. Here stood another fine medieval house, Parlwr Mawr, where John Williams was born in 1582. He became Archbishop of York in 1641 and was a strong supporter of the crown during the Civil War. He repaired the castle and garrisoned the town at his own expense. During the conflict however, he switched sides after his loyalty was not reciprocated by King Charles, and assisted Parliamentary forces in gaining control of the town. Parlwr Mawr survived until 1948 when it was demolished for safety reasons when no public body accepted responsibility for its restoration.

The Tudor kitchen at Plas Mawr

The crest of the Welsh prince, Owain Gwynedd in a Plas Mawr ceiling

Colourful plasterwork

The estuary port of Conwy

Fishermen still bring their catches to the quay

A river port

The monks of Abaty Aberconwy were granted ferry rights on the estuary by the princes of Gwynedd; the kings of England later demanded these for their own exchequer and for centuries it was the only way to cross the river. Since the days when Conwy was an isolated English outpost, navigation ensured that a life-line supply of military assistance and essential goods was always within reach. The quay was paramount to the existence of the town, and in peaceful times it grew as a sea harbour for inland goods. In Tudor times, an unusual number of Conwy town houses were roofed with slate – but that is not surprising on realising that slate, and later lead and zinc, were shipped downstream in small boats from Trefriw quay, before being loaded on larger vessels. This continued into the early part of the 20th century.

Dyffryn Conwy is rich in oak trees. Between 1754-1760 alone, £50,000 worth of best oak was floated down from Gwydir estate for the shipwrights. Sloops and schooners were built for the coastal trade, carrying copper from Gogarth mines to Abertawe (*Swansea*) bringing coal on the return journey. Potatoes and corn were explorted to Liverpool; wheat to Ireland and oatmeal to Scotland and bark for the tanning industry.

The Liverpool Arms on Conwy quay was a favourite haunt of Conwy mariners. In the 1830's, the landlord was a certain Captain Jones who also ran a steamer, the Conwy Castle, backwards and forwards between the quay and Liverpool. It covered the 45-mile trip in five hours and also took foot passengers – five shillings down below or half a crown up on the deck.

When Telford improved the road communications and built an embankment to reach the rocky island from which he suspended his famous bridge, it caused silting upriver. Llansanffraid Glan Conwy lost its significance as a river port but allowed Conwy to thrive on the lost trade. The Conwy wooden quay was rebuilt by four stonemasons in 1831 and their efforts still stand the floods and the tides under the town walls to this day. Conwy's shipping fortunes was soon to be diminished by the arrival of the railway however, which reached to town in 1849.

Pleasure-seekers provided trade for a different kind of boat however. In their heyday, elegant paddle steamers ferried travellers from Conwy and Deganwy to Trefriw. The service lasted from 1847 to 1940 and it took an hour and a half to make the journey up the tidal river, carriying up to 170 passengers. The tall black funnels of the steamers had special hinges to allow them to fold down to pass beneath the Conwy suspension bridge. The trips were finally ceased when warplanes used Dyffryn Conwy for their return flights after bombing Liverpool – river traffic was thought too risky under the circumstances. Smaller paddles continued in the 1950's and today boats still run river cruises from Conwy quay.

The recently extended quay

Fishermen at work

Restoring a traditional 150 year old Conwy Nobby Prawner on the quay

Conwy is still renowned for its mussel fishermen

An old postcard showing mussel and salmon boats

Salmon and mussels

Conwy fish has been feasted on with relish since time immemorial. An old Irish manuscript relates how St Bridget landed near Deganwy castle after an adventurous crossing from Ireland. According to local legend, she found the people here starving after seasons of bad weather. She threw a handful of reeds into the estuary which immediately turned into long, green-like fish which were fed to the population. The saint, called Ffraid in Welsh, established her chapel at Llansanffraid Glan Conwy, and the migratory fish – brwyniad ('*reed fish*' or sparling/smelt) is still fished with two boats and a seine net on Afon Conwy in late March and early April.

Another legend tells of a mermaid who was stranded on a large stone in the estuary. She asked a group of fishermen to save her and throw her back into the sea. They laughed at her plight, but when the tide finally turned and freed her she cursed them as she swam back to the sea. When losses at sea have befallen Conwy, some still think back to the mermaid's words.

Salmon used to be caught in the river also, in the abbey weirs on the eastern side using the old Welsh method – netting with coracles. These had a framework of laths covered with canvas, tightly stretched and coated with pitch to make them water-tight. They are very light vessels, easily carried on the back of one man and are still used on three rivers in southern Wales. Salmon netting is still allowed in the estuary but only a few licences remain, inherited from one generation to another within the fishing families of Conwy.

Deep-sea fisherman still bring back catches of plaice and cod to Conwy quay, but the town is probably more famous for its mussels than any other seafood. The gathering of 'Cregyn Gleision', the edible blue mussel, goes back as an industry to the 1840's – again the fast railway connections with the populated towns was a key factor. At one time the shells supported 40 full-time fishermen.

The mussels are found in abundance in sandbeds on the bar at the mouth of the river and were gathered daily by men, women and children at ebb-tide. The fishermen had long-handled net-rakes which were used to raise the harvest until the returning tide drove them away. The shells wee then carried in sacks and baskets to Cefnfro on Morfa Conwy where they were boiled in iron pots and prepared for market.

Gathering mussels as seafood became more profitable eventually – the tradition methods remained the same: handpicking in the shallows and raking the deeper pools. The Ministry of Agriculture and Fisheries stepped in with its regulations eventually and purification tanks were installed at the mouth of Afon Gyffin, upstream of the castle. Modern equipment are now used and the Conwy Cragen Las is as tasty as ever and can be bought from the fish stall at the quay.

Past Conwy mussel fishermen

Sacks of mussels on their way to the purification tanks, ready for the market

The Conwy Mussel Museum and heritage sculpture

An old print of Conwy ferry boats

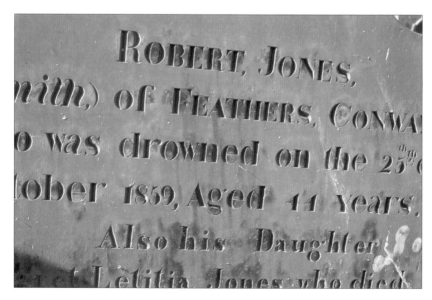

ROBERT JONES,
(...ith,) of FEATHERS, CONWA...
...o was drowned on the 25ᵗʰ...
...tober 1859, Aged 44 years.
Also his Daughter...
...et Letitia Jones who died...

A reminder of the perils of Conwy waters in St Mary's graveyard

By coach, by ferry

In the eighteenth century, any stranger travelling from Chester to Bangor needed a guide to help him reach the Conwy estuary, cross it safely and then negotiate the tidal perils and precipitous narrow paths. Even guides and ferrymen lost their lives.

Individual travellers and the mailcoach started to use the northern coastal road. The Conwy Races attracted huge crowds to the Morfa until 1794 and Conwy fairs were renown far and wide. Hyde Hall wrote of the display of fruit offered for sale – peaches, nectarines and grapes were grown within the walls which possessed 'a flavour and a richness superior' to any found elsewhere.

Conwy hostelries, however, had a bad reputation but even early authors mention a few good inns. *The King's Head* (now a part of the Castle Hotel), *Red Lion, Bull, Eagles, Swan* and *Harp* are all registered before 1769. As the eighteenth century progressed, travel increased on the 'Great Irish Road', as the coastal road was called, even though the state of the roads and ferries were designed for horseback journeys. In 1753, no less than eight horse-drawn coaches left Chester for Caergybi (*Holyhead*) within 48 hours. Conwy became a compulsory stop for horse-changing and waiting for the correct conditions. The larger carriages could not manage the steep climb to Sychnant and the sharp fall to Dwygyfylchi and had to tackle the sands around Penmaen-bach and Penmaen-mawr at ebb-tide. The tides were dangerous, the estuary was muddy and the banks hid treacherous quicksand underfoot. Coaches overturned and got bogged down.

Up to the first half of the twentieth century, half a dozen ferrymen were still operating across the narrow river mouth opposite Deganwy. There was a ferry point here since medieval times, but when the coaching days arrived the coach was carried on large, flat-bottomed ferryboats which crossed from where is now called 'Glan Conwy corner'. These were clumsy and could not always cross the estuary. Passengers had to wait for hours in the Conwy taverns for their coach to follow them.

The ferrymen were also notorious for overcharging. Foot passengers usually paid a penny each, but coach travellers were required to pay a shilling each. It was an unpleasant journey in every sense and alternative routes were sought for. Some saw it worthwhile to travel upriver to the old Roman fort of Caerhun, and cross by the Tal-y-cafn ferry. An inland coach road was developed from Shrewsbury to Llanrwst, which later headed through the Eryri mountains via Capel Curig to Bangor.

Disaster struck the Conwy ferry on Christmas Day, 1806 – the ferryboat carrying the Irish Mail capsized with the loss of 13 lives. At the moment when there was real danger that Conwy was going to be by-passed, the public outcry resulted in new plans for a bridge to cross the estuary to be drawn out.

The 'bell' was used to call the ferryman

50

Sychnant Pass –
the old coach road to Anglesey

Penmaenbach
from Morfa Conwy

The tradition of welcoming travellers is maintained in
Conwy's inns and hotels

The three bridges and the embankment

The Telford suspension bridge

Bridging Conwy waters

The Act of Union of Ireland and England in 1801 brought influencial travellers to tackle the journey from Caergybi (*Holyhead*) and London. The question of crossing the Conwy estuary became an international matter, and a bridge was called for.

Conwy had been built so that the river was a natural barrier to the town. The time had come to make the town more accessible and the colonialisation of Ireland this time gave Conwy a new breath of life.

Thomas Telford was already engineering two roads across northern Wales – the A5 from Shrewsbury through the mountains to Bangor and the A55 from Chester, following the coast to Bangor. The original concept was an arched bridge, connected from a rocky island opposite Conwy castle to the eastern side by an embankment. This cob, a third of a mile long, was created with picks and shovels in an intense battle against the river and sea currents. This was revised when Telford started on the Menai suspension bridge in 1819. Telford's Conwy suspension bridge was completed in 1826, after taking four years to build. It would be the only crossing for vehicles and pedestrians for 133 years. Its span is 327 feet (98 m), its towers blend in with the castle backdrop, which also anchors the weight of the suspended deck of the bridge. A road was cut into the north-eastern side of the castle rock and new and noble gateway was constructed to the town. The bridge is now National Trust property and the tollkeeper's house has recently been restored and furnished as it would have been in 1900.

Traffic through Conwy increased dramatically. During the nineteenth century, Conwy's fortunes took an upward leap. The population boomed from 889 to 5,240 and taverns, shops and merchants were doing a roaring trade. The great flourish is reflected in a tiny house on the quay side: in 1800, it was an 'in-fill' fisherman cottage between two terraces, only 72 inches (1.8m) wide; by the time the terrace on one side was pulled down in 1900, it was a Victorian tourist attraction open to the many who came to enjoy the town by then buying, among other things, postcards of the 'Smallest House in Britain'.

Twenty years after Telford's suspension bridge, the iron steam engines crossed the Conwy embankment. Giant steel tubes were constructed near the Gyffin stream estuary, engineered by Robert Stephenson; stone supporting-towers were erected and six wooden pontoons were used to float the 312 feet (94 m) long massive tubes, each weighing 1,300 tons, to their lifting stations. Again the Conwy tubular railway bridge is a lesser companion to a similar structure crossing Afon Menai, taking the railway line onwards for the Irish ferry port. The first stone was laid in 1846 and both railway lines were operational by 1849. Stephenson, like Telford, had to breach the town walls for his new route which he later bridged with an elegant skewed arch near the railway station.

The tollhouse on the suspension bridge

The tubular railway bridge

The Conwy suspension bridge before the road bridge

Morfa Conwy

The first golf course in Wales – Caernarfonshire Golf Club on the Morfa

Morfa Conwy

Conwy is fronted by the river and backed by the mountains. To the north-east is a wooded knoll, with low-lying grassland and dunes beyond. This area of sand, sea and marsh, the Morfa, was part of Edward I's grant of land to the thirteenth century Borough. Over the years the Morfa has been exploited for a variety of civil and military purposes whilst the hilly land on its south-eastern fringe was developed as a park and mansion in the eighteenth century. The area provides stunning river, estuary and marine views.

Conwy Morfa has provided useful grazing land for the town since at least the foundation of Aberconwy Abbey in the twelfth century. Every burgess with a house or land in Conwy was permitted to graze animals on the Morfa, but had to pay the Town Corporation for the privilege. A Marsh Warden, or Keeper, was appointed and attempts at unwarranted intrusion were swiftly dealt with. In the seventeenth century typical charges were four shillings for a horse and two shillings each for cattle, for three months grazing.

The Morfa was also the venue for the annual Conwy Race Meeting and it is now the site of the Conwy United Football Club ground. Football has officially been played on the Morfa since at least 1894 when Conwy originally applied to join the new North Wales Coast Football Association. In 1903 the club were in trouble when the referee of their match against Porthmadog complained that he had been 'under threat from the Conwy crowd of 200 to 300 supporters'!

The Morfa also hosts probably Wales' first golf course. The 10th April 1903 issue of *Golf Illustrated* claimed that 'It is well authenticated that in 1869 three enthusiastic gentlemen hailing from Scotland laid out a nine-hole golf course on Conwy Morfa'. In 1876 Jack Morris, the club professional of the Royal Liverpool improved the course on behalf of a group of members who regularly holidayed in Conwy. Unfortunately both parties neglected to have found a separate club organisation to administer this new course. By the time that local players eventually got around to doing this in 1890 they had been pipped at the post by both Tenby, (founded, November 1888) and Rhyl, (March 1890). The founding meeting of the Caernarfonshire Golf Club eventually took place in Conwy Guildhall on June 30th, 1890. The club and its Morfa course swiftly secured a good reputation, and in 1899 hosted the Welsh Amateur Golf Championships. The Welsh Professional Championship followed in 1905. Over the years the club has seen its course and its clubhouses fall victim to the adverse effects of fire, the army and the Expressway, but has adapted and survived to celebrate its centenary.

(extracts from *Walks from Conwy*, Christopher Draper)

Camping on the Morfa

On the greens at Morfa Conwy

The estuary and the beach at the Morfa

The railway at Conwy

The Mulberry Harbour in the estuary

The tunnel and the marina

Better lines of communication had an effect on the future development of the northern Wales coast. It soon became fashionable to trip to the seaside from the industrial towns and cities. Lancashire and Deeside factory workers soon flocked to Welsh beaches and spas for health and leisure reasons. With the railroad, Llandudno sprang into existence overnight in 1850's and was a major resort by the 1880's. Colwyn Bay developed in 1890's. For a while, Conwy and the immediate area were served well by the railroad network.

In the 1920's and 30's however, the sudden increase in the use of motor vehicles had a dramatic effect on the narrow streets of the town centre. The toll on the suspension bridge created lengthy queues and there were plans for a motor route that would have destroyed Conwy's quay. Eventually a new road bridge opened in 1958, sweeping the traffic problem right through the centre of the town, creating even more congestion and making the old streets miserable for everybody.

The planners went to work again and in the interest of heritage and conservation the Conwy estuary tunnel was finally accepted as inevitable, Conwy was to be freed of its 5 mile tailbacks every holiday weekend as the northern coast road – now upgraded to a double carriageway and recognised as a major European international link – would by-pass one of the finest examples of medieval walled towns.

The estuary was on the world engineering map once again as the first immersed tube tunnel was built and lowered into the river bed. Six reinforced concrete units were fabricated on the Morfa – a site which had forty years previously seen the large-scale building of Mulberry Harbours for the Normandy landings of the Second World War. The excavated basin on the Morfa side of the estuary – this was eventually flooded and the concrete sections were floated precisely into place in a deep trench that had been dredged in the river bed. In May 1900, a great sponsored walk marked the opening of a tunnel which was as remarkable and historic engineering feat as any that the shores of Conwy had seen over the ages.

A by-product of the floating sections was a flooded basin on Morfa Conwy. The estuary had long harboured pleasure boats and sailing yachts, side by side as the working fishing fleet of Conwy. Now the leisure boats would have their own moorings in a new purpose built marina on the Morfa. This was further developed to include accommodation, shops and an inn.

On the other side of the old Conwy embankment, the mud flats on the eastern bank had been filled in with the large amount of spoil that came out of the trench in the river bed. This was reclaimed and landscaped as a reed-fringed lagoon and an RSPB reserve was established here in 1993. It matured and attracted birds rapidly. It now has a visitor centre, picnic area, birdwatching hides, nature trails and a wealth of wildlife under the dramatic scenery of Snowdonia and the Conwy estuary.

The marina basin was created when the A55 tunnel
under the estuary was built

Moorings and quayside housing at the marina

The RSPB centre on the estuary

River cruises and the Smallest House on the quay

Welsh produce at its best at Edwards of Conwy butchers

64

Walking with history

The Marine Walk downstream from Conwy quay runs along the water's edge, bordering on the old pleasure gardens of a mansion (Bodlondeb) built by a member of a local prominent family in 1742. The quay itself has many attractions to locals and visitors, including fresh catches by the fishermen.

The life in the town goes on. The Welsh, categorised as 'foreigners' and excluded when the town was founded, have long made it their own. The typical terrace cottages and high chapels have stamped their style on the old fortress colony and its culture became one with that of the surrounding valleys. When John Wesley visited the town in 1754, he met whole families that were monolingual speakers – their whole lives were lived through the Welsh language. Conwy natives, born within the town walls, are familiarly known as 'jackdaws' by the valley people.

In 1851, a national three-day eisteddfod was held inside Conwy castle. Poets, harpists, vocalists submerged the town in a festival of music and literature and the atmosphere was surely similar to that of Maelgwn's old competition on Mynydd y Dre, a millennium earlier. Special railway trains brought masses of followers from all over Wales to the town and the town's arms adorned the castle wall, proudly carrying the motto 'Oes y byd i'r iaith Gymraeg' ('*Long live the Welsh language*').

Welsh food and Welsh crafts today bring a new kind of commercialism to the town that has recently benefited from re-paving roads surfaces in the wake of solving its traffic problems – it has kept its integrity as a market town, offering the best of its culture without selling its soul in pieces of souvenirs. It displays its medieval grandeur with pride, proud also that its Welsh culture has survived the military attempt at its extinction. Visitors flock to its walls, its quay, its castle and its streets from every part of Europe and America, admiring it as a World Heritage Site, enjoying its atmosphere and its ability to absorb other cultures without losing its own. It is still very much a lived in town, not a walled open-air museum (information: *www.conwy.gov.uk*). Business is as usual; the marina may be for pleasure but Conwy quay is still a working fishing port.

Upriver, Bodnant Gardens, now in the care of the National Trust, is a major attraction and was established in 1875 on a south facing hill above Afon Conwy, near Eglwysbach. It is a world-famous garden, noted for its botanical collections and panoramic views of the valley and the Carneddau mountains. Created by five generations of one family, this 32-hectare (80-acre) garden is superbly located with plants from all over the world. With expansive lawns and intimate corners, grand ponds and impressive terraces, a steep wooded valley and stream, as well as awe-inspiring plant collections, there are continually changing glorious displays of colour.

Nearby, the Bodnant Welsh Food Centre is located at Furnace Farm, in the stunning surroundings of the Conwy Valley. Originally built in the 18th century, the buildings have been lovingly restored to provide an excellent venue for a farm shop, tea room, restaurant, cookery school and farmhouse accommodation. It also houses a National Beekeeping Centre for Wales, a bakery, a cheese factory and ice-cream dairy.

From parapet walks to river cruises, from pony trekking on Mynydd y Dre to meandering through the narrow streets of the town centre, Conwy still offers more than another outing on another holiday. Memory is embodied in the masonry; stories meet you on the streets. Its past has certainly seen turmoil and opression, but the present has been able to find and display its own pride in its original roots, accepting the empty shell of Edward I's military garrison as a tribute to native resolve and endurance.

Bodnant Gardens

Bodnant Welsh Food Centre

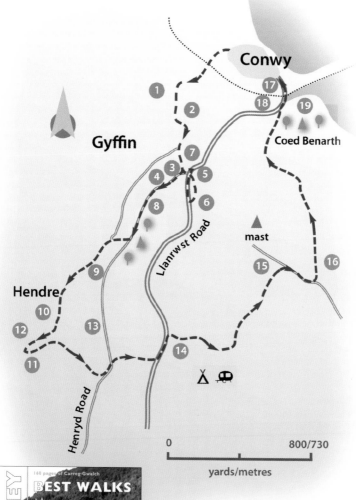

Conwy

17
18
19

Coed Benarth

Gyffin

1
2
7
3
4
5
8
6

Llanrwst Road

▲
mast

15
16

Hendre

9
10
13
12
11
14

⛺ 🚐

Henryd Road

0   800/730

yards/metres

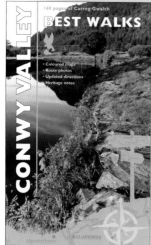

Walk selected from:

Carreg Gwalch Best Walks in the Conwy Valley

A Walk from Conwy
Beyond the Pale in the Parish of Gyffin

Walk details
Approx distance: *4 miles/6.4 kilometres*

Approx time: *2½-3 hours*

O.S. Maps: *1:50 000 Landranger Sheet 115*
                1:25 000 Explorer OL17

Start: *Llywelyn's Monument, Lancaster Square, Conwy.*
                Grid Ref. SH 781 776

Access: *Conwy town centre.*

Parking: *Park by the castle wall, 300 yards from town centre. Pay and*
                display car park.

Going: *Quiet country lanes and field paths.*

Introduction
Edward I's Conwy was an English town, with the Welsh forced to live 'beyond the pale', to move across the river which protected the southern flank of the town. South of this boundary they might be tolerated, north of the river they might be killed. This river was the border, which in Welsh is *cyffin*, mutated to *gyffin*. Nine hundred years later it is still known as Afon Gyffin, and the parish itself is called Gyffin. This walk explores the parish 'beyond the pale' and uncovers more recent repercussions of culture clash and exclusivity.

The Walk and Points of Interest
From Llywelyn's monument, walk north-east along Bangor Road. Once through the walls turn left along Mount Pleasant, then right,

69

ascending Sychnant Pass road for 100 yards (90m). Turn left along the path by the footpath (1) sign.

1.   Bryn Corach was built as a private house, in an attractive 'Scots-Baronial meets Conwy Castle' style of architecture. Since 1913 it has been owned and run by the Holiday Fellowship. HF grew out of the movement to provide access to the countryside for city-dwellers who had been increasingly deprived of the joys of nature by the relentless march of Victorian industrialisation. The founder of HF was T. A. Leonard, a non-conformist minister from Lancashire. Known as the 'father of the open-air movement', he began by organising holiday schemes as an extension of his church's rambling club. He formed the Co-Operative Holidays Association' in 1891 and the Holiday Fellowship in 1913. Leonard personally chose Bryn Corach as a holiday centre and headquarters but was supported by an equally determined and idealistic committee, which included the influential Tolstoyan, Percy Redfern. The idealistic companionship offered by the Fellowship soon attracted progressive figures, like Bernard Shaw, to stay at Bryn Corach but when war broke out in 1914 the HF commitment to international friendship and peace was resented by local 'jingos'. Armed men were constantly banging on the front door and accusing Bryn Corach residents of flashing torches in an attempt to communicate with the enemy. The authorities were also determined to 'get Bryn Corach' but couldn't manage to prove anything until one day the dried fruit ration for three other holiday centres was delivered here by mistake. Leonard and Miss Brothers, the manageress of Bryn Corach were both summoned to appear at Conwy Police Court, prosecuted for 'hoarding food' and fined £10! Not all Conwy residents were antagonistic and many admired HF's generosity in housing Belgian refugees. The idealism continues and holiday fellowship is still available at Bryn Corach.

Continue through the metal gate and down the lane, which curves to the left and passes a short terrace of houses (2), before joining St Agnes Road, where you turn right.

2. These houses were erected in the hollow of a worked-out Victorian quarry. Stone was extracted from here in the 1870s to consolidate and repair Conwy castle's Bakehouse Tower, courtesy of Francis G. Jones (1816-1889), the owner of the Bryn Corach Estate.

Continue as the road bears left, cross at the school sign and follow the footpath on the right as it descends the bank, crosses a metal footbridge and arrives at an ancient church (3) and churchyard (4).

3. The foundation of St Benedict's church is a bit of a mystery. The most plausible theory is that it was built in the early 13th century by the Cistercian monks of Aberconwy to serve local people whilst they reserved their abbey chapel mainly for their own use and for the devotions of their illustrious guests. It is possible, however, that the monks merely rededicated an existing church here or even that Gyffin church was built to serve the local Welsh population only after they had been expelled from Aberconwy by Edward I. If the monks did indeed build this church, it seems logical that it was dedicated to that great founder of Latin monasticism, Saint Benedict, but even here it is not so straight-forward as the Cistercians more usually dedicated their churches to Mary. Whatever the details of its foundation, by the 15th century it was already considered necessary to extend the church to cater for local people who were still excluded from town life and worship. Yet even the extensive Victorian 'improvements' of 1858 haven't entirely destroyed the ancient character of St Benedict's. Inside there is an extremely unusual 15th century painted celure, or canopy, whilst outside the porch is especially interesting. The attractive

St Benedict's church at Gyffin

timber frame of the porch is 14th century, whilst the 13th century memorial stone set into the porch's left flank provides another intriguing mystery. This slightly tapering memorial stone, which can be viewed from the outside through the wooden mullions, seems to bear the inscription: HIC IACAT LLYWELYN AP IORWERTH. Could this be part of the gravestone of the founder of Aberconwy salvaged by loyal Welshmen and women when Edward ordered his body be removed from Conwy?

4. There are several other monuments scattered around St Benedict's churchyard that are worth seeking out. A large, slate table-top stone marking a family grave, behind the church, includes a memorial to 'Owen Williams, engineer of the Mail Steamer *Inca* in the Pacific Ocean who died at Tobogo (*sic*) on 29 September, 1859, aged 28'. Near the church porch, to the east of the path lie two gardeners, Richard Owen and Hugh Roberts, who worked at Benarth Hall, of which you will hear more later. Under the branches of the large tree near the gate, to the west of the path, lies Elizabeth, wife of Thomas Williams, of the Foresters' Arms, Gyffin, which we will visit after I first explain how just over a century ago this churchyard achieved a certain

notoriety. It began at 3.45 p.m. on Saturday 3 May, 1890 as the funeral procession of William Williams passed the spot where you are now standing. As the 'venerable white-haired, surpliced Rector Thomas Ellis entered the church, book in hand' the following mourners and coffin-bearers wheeled off to the left and ignoring the absence of the rector proceeded to lower the deceased into an open grave attended by a Welsh Wesleyan Minister. 'Suddenly becoming aware that no-one was following him the Rector rushed out of the church shouting.' Amidst the tears and hymn singing of the mourning family at the graveyard, the Gyffin rector who was a Conwy curate, and the Wesleyan minister began haranguing each other. The rector refused to allow the rites of the Wesleyan Conference to take place and the deceased was eventually laid to rest without any formal funeral service taking place, or any memorial stone being erected. In the ensuing publicity the rector claimed that the deceased hadn't been entitled to be buried in Gyffin as he had lived in Conwy parish, but this had not disqualified others from burial here. The real explanation is more complex for 'The Gyffin Burial Sensation' was but a single, particularly public and dramatic skirmish in a long-running and widespread battle between the established church and non-conformity.

Leave the churchyard through the main gate, turn left and when you reach the Llanrwst Road, cross to the tiny house (5) on the opposite corner. Then ascent Llanrwst Road to the first house (6) before descending again, continuing across the road and over the bridge to the chip shop (7).

5. Turnpike Cottage has a stone set into the front gable that records its erection in 1930, during the reign of King William IV. The resident toll-collector was responsible for collecting the fees from travellers along this section of the Caernarfonshire Turnpike Road, which led from Llanrwst to Pwllheli. This was officially listed as 'gate number 2', with Gwydir, near Llanrwst as

'number 1'. The Trust didn't actually operate the gates themselves, preferring to lease them out, on an annual basis, to the highest bidder. The greatest annual amount ever collected in tolls here amounted to £108, in 1850, when John Hughes was the resident collector. The standard tolls charged were 2d. each for non-draught horses, 10d. per score of cattle in droves whilst pigs, sheep and geese were charged at 5d. a score. In 1882 the Trust expired on the adoption of the road by the local authority, all tolls ceased and the tollhouse and gate were sold off. The house fetched £80 before being resold to Robert Rowlands, the miller.

6. Notice the blank plaque which adorns the front wall above the door. A hundred years ago this bore the name of the Foresters' Arms (remember the gravestone reference?), for this was the village inn. The metal trapdoor leading down to the old beer-cellar can still be seen at street level, to the left of the front door, and the old brew-house remains in the back yard but the licence was withdrawn almost a century ago. Local opinion traces this misfortune back to the time of Queen Victoria's funeral in 1901. The local authority asked all local businesses to close for the day as a mark of respect, but the Foresters' are believed to have been the only public house in Britain to have remained open and so lost their licence as a consequence! Unfortunately the truth is more routine, the Foresters' operated until 1903 and was eventually closed down because it offered limited facilities to bona fide travellers but rather unlimited facilities to drunks! The landlord simply ran a disorderly house, brawling was a speciality, and his licence was withdrawn as a result.

7. This was Gyffin corn mill, powered by water flowing from a pond at the rear, now filled in. Water was delivered via a long mill-race that branched off Afon Gyffin, upstream. The mill pond was contained by a mill-dam and crossed by a little bridge that

originally carried the footpath that you previously followed to reach the church. The miller's house stands between the chip shop and Afon Gyffin.

Retrace your steps to the church gate before continuing along Henryd Road for 400 yards (360m) until you reach the old stone-built rectory (8), on the left.

8. This impressive residence was the home of the Reverend Thomas Robert Ellis of 'Burial Scandal' fame. Ellis was appointed to Gyffin parish as a curate in 1852 and formally appointed as Rector on 19 January, 1953. He was succeeded by Robert Jones in 1898. The Reverend Jones had thirteen children and his relatives always considered that the Bishop of Bangor offered him this situation as the large rectory seemed particular suitable for accommodating his ever increasing family! In 1925 Gyffin lost the status of maintaining its own rector and the rectory was subsequently sold off and converted to accommodate holidaymakers.

After a further 400 yards (360m) you reach a lone house, on the right, where you descend three steps and follow a footpath over a footbridge. Bear left and on reaching the road turn left and continue for 200 yards (180m) to Tyddyn Melus (9), a white painted cottage on the left.

9. Tyddyn Melus is a delight, a largely original 18th century cottage of a type that was once common in north Wales. Notice the huge, characteristic projecting corner boulders.

Continuing in the same direction you soon reach a long terraced building alongside a T-junction (10). Continue ahead for another 200 yards (180m) to Hen Bodidda (11), on the left with a more modern farmhouse Henllys (12), on the right.

10.A century ago these buildings contained the blacksmith shop of Jabez Jones. Jabez learned the craft from Thomas, his father, a native of Llanrhos. Later in this walk I will point out an example of their Victorian handiwork.

11. Bodidda was built around 1550 by Hugh Stodart but within a hundred years it had passed into the ownership of the Owen family, with whom it is usually associated. The building was once one of the major houses of the area and although it has declined in importance something of its former status is signalled by the presence of the bell suspended in the gable end. This indicates an establishment employing a large number of farmhands who would be rung in from their widely distributed tasks in the fields at meal times.

12. Henllys, originally Halesfield, makes an interesting contrast with Bodidda. Almost three hundred and fifty years younger, it was built more as a gentleman's country residence rather than a functional farmhouse. The prominent monkey-puzzle tree is a period sign of social pretension. Trees were traditionally planted to provide fruit and timber and shade for animals, or windbreaks for farmhouses. A monkey-puzzle announces that the owner has interests above such mundane concerns, sophisticated and exotic taste and is, in a word, a gentleman. Sadly maintaining social pretension can be stressful and in 1928 led to terrible consequences at Henllys. Retired, and respectable farmer, David Owen lived here with his wife in what were described at the time as 'comfortable circumstances'. The couple employed domestic staff and had no money worries but Mr Owen became convinced that he was in decline, physically, socially and financially and 'would be better off in the workhouse'. On the morning of Wednesday, 4 January, Eluned, the maid, served Mr Owen his breakfast, as usual. He then went out and as he hadn't returned for lunch, Eluned went to look for him. Finding him in the coach-house she sought the assistance of neighbour Richard

Roberts of Bodidda. Richard explained that having been called to Henllys coach-house he found David Owen, 'lying in a pool of blood, face downwards. His two sticks were in his hand, and on the ground near him was an open razor'. The Coroner's verdict was, 'Suicide in a fit of depression'.

Retrace your steps as far as the council houses, where you turn right, descend the green and continue down the road. Cross Pont Gyffredin, turning left at the junction and continuing to Cyffredin, where you ascend the footpath opposite through the kissing gate. Pause at the first wooden field gate on the left and glance down at the huge ruin (13), to the right of Cyffredin, before continuing past an attractive old cottage to soon reach the roadway, going through two kissing gates on your way.

13. This was a candle factory whose products were highly regarded by local lead miners. Being tallow candles, they tended to drip much less than wax alternatives. Owen Owen, the candlemaker here in the 1880s and 1890s used to collect skins from slaughterhouses in Conwy and Penmaenmawr and deposit them at his depot behind the Harp Inn, Conwy, on the site of the old Woolworth's on High Street. When he had stripped off the fat he would employ his horse and cart to deliver it here for processing. Once inside the factory, the crude animal fat was chopped up, rendered down, clarified and poured into dipping troughs. Meanwhile the wicks were cut to the desired lengths, attached to a rod suspended over the trough and then the hanging wicks were dipped into the molten tallow before being removed and allowed to cool. This process was then repeated several times until the desired thickness of candle was reached. Llywelyn Evans took over from Owen but gradually the decline in local mining, the increasing efficiency of oil lamps and the greater availability of electricity together conspired to reduce

the demand for candles. The factory closed during the First World War.

Turn left, after 200 yards (180m) follow the footpath signs through 'Conwy Touring Park' past Bryn Hyfryd (14). Half way up the hill go through the kissing gate, next to the public footpath sign. Follow the footpath signs through two kissing gates. Cross the campsite lane, follow the track ahead. Ignore the first stile on your right, head for the stile in front of you. Head up the hill, keep going for 700 yards (640m), keeping with the right hand side of several fields. You will go through three kissing gates, before coming to a minor road.

14.   In Victorian times Bryn Hyfryd was the home of William Hughes, the local postman. In the years between the growth of motorised transport and the widespread adoption of private transport, rural postmen helped keep open traditional rights of way. Before being supplied with vans postmen walked from farm to farm along these centuries-old footpaths whilst completing their daily deliveries.

15. Look carefully at the nameplate attached to the top of the metal gate, it reads 'Jabez Jones, maker of Hendre'; you visited his Victorian smithy at (10).

Turn right, after 200 yards (180m) cross the ladder stile on the left and follow the field path past Home Farm (16).

16. This is the Home Farm of the Benarth Estate, which established a legal monopoly over the whole one hundred and thirty-five acres that lie between you and Afon Conwy. At the heart of the estate and hidden from public view stands Benarth

Hall, a magnificent Georgian country house of 1790, possibly the work of John Nash. The mansion was created for Samuel Price of Lincoln's Inn but sold by his executors in June 1805. The sale particulars described the house as: 'An elegant, commodious and modern built mansion house, suitable for a large family and with every description of offices'. It included 'beautiful pleasure grounds laid out with great taste and enriched with forest trees and the choicest evergreens', as well as a 'hot house, green house, pinery, melon pit, peachery and ice house'. The estate is still the preserve of wealthy owners and you are prohibited from walking down to the river, strolling through the pleasure grounds, or even allowing your gaze to alight upon that elegant and commodious mansion.

Continue over a series of ladder stiles and across fields for 800 yards (730m) before bearing left along the hedge, as indicated by a footpath arrow sign. Soon you enter the south-western fringe of Benarth Woods. Following the descending path, you soon emerge atop a steep bank with a panoramic view of Conwy ahead. Before descending to the road glance over at the second castle tower (17) from the railway bridge.

17. The contrasting stonework of the Bakehouse Tower and its buttress is evidence of extensive Victorian repair work. The rock on which the tower was constructed had disintegrated causing a huge section of the tower to collapse. Curiously, the top section remained intact but below that a yawning gap stretched almost the full length of the tower; the image was captured in a painting by Turner. As the railway runs along this southern flank of the castle, the London and North Western Railway Company agreed to stabilise and repair the tower at their own expense. The work was completed in April 1881.

Afon Gyffin and Conwy castle

Turn right along Llanrwst Road, passing the garage (18) on the left before crossing the bridge over the Gyffin stream (19) and turning left alongside the Guildhall to return along Rose Hill to Lancaster Square.

18. A century ago this was Peter and Humphrey Lewis' timber yard and steam saw mill. Humphrey was also a Conwy Councillor who lived at Muriau, which you pass, on your right, next to the former National School, as you return along Rose Hill.

19. Afon Gyffin formerly carried a much greater volume of water and was much wider at this point. The waters of Afon Gyffin lapped against the lower walls of the castle until the railway company altered its course to allow for the convenient laying of track and the creation of a goods yard (note the surviving railway crane). In the Middle Ages the Welsh were permitted to harbour their ships and receive supplies here, but they were not allowed to use the Conwy-town quay.